The Gray Whale

by Cynthia Swain

Scott Foresman
is an imprint of

Glenview, Illinois • Boston, Massachusetts • Chandler, Arizona
Upper Saddle River, New Jersey

Photo locators denoted as follows: Top (T), Center (C), Bottom (B), Left (L), Right (R), Background (Bkgd)

Opener: (C) Hiroya MInakuchi/Minden Pictures,(Bkgd) Brand X Pictures; 1 DK Images; 3 DK Images; 4 (C, T) DK Images, (Bkgd) ©Steve Wilkings/Corbis; 5 (CL) Getty Images, (BL) Hiroya Minakuchi/Minden Pictures, (R) Staffan Widstrand/Corbis; 6 DK Images; 7 DK Images; 8 (BL) DK Images, (C) Getty Images, (B) Flip Nicklin/Minden Pictures; 9 (C) Hiroya MInakuchi/Minden Pictures, (T) DK Images; 10 (C) Flip Nicklin/Minden Pictures, (B) Minden Pictures; 11 Neil Rabinowitz/Corbis; 13 Frans Lanting/Minden Pictures; 14 Konrad Wothe/Minden Pictures; 15 Getty Images

ISBN 13: 978-0-328-51646-9
ISBN 10:   0-328-51646-5

4 5 6 7 8 9 10 V0FL 15 14 13 12 11

TABLE OF CONTENTS

CHAPTER 1   4

Meet the gray whale!

CHAPTER 2   6

What do gray whales look like?

CHAPTER 3   10

How do gray whales eat?

CHAPTER 4   12

How do gray whales migrate?

CHAPTER 5   14

How do gray whales communicate?

Glossary   16

CHAPTER ONE
Meet the gray whale!

The **massive**, gray creature slowly raises its head out of the water. It seems to take a look around. Then it sinks below the surface. That whale is spy hopping. Marine **biologists,** or scientists who study ocean life, believe that gray whales may use spy hopping to see where they are. But no one is really sure why whales spy hop.

This gray whale is spy hopping.

There are about eighty different kinds of whales. Gray whales spend most of their lives fairly close to shore. Scientists have been able to observe these whales more easily than whales that spend their lives in the deep ocean.

Gray whales came close to extinction because of too much hunting. Extinction is when a species dies out. People thought that gray whales should not become extinct. In 1946, hunting gray whales was stopped. There are now more than twenty-five thousand gray whales in the eastern Pacific Ocean.

A gray whale surfaces.

People enjoy touching a gray whale.

CHAPTER TWO

What do gray whales look like?

Gray whales are named for their color. They are mostly gray. Their bodies are also covered in patches of white and yellow. These patches are caused by whale lice and barnacles. Barnacles and whale lice are small creatures that live on the whale's skin. There can be one hundred pounds of whale lice and barnacles on one gray whale!

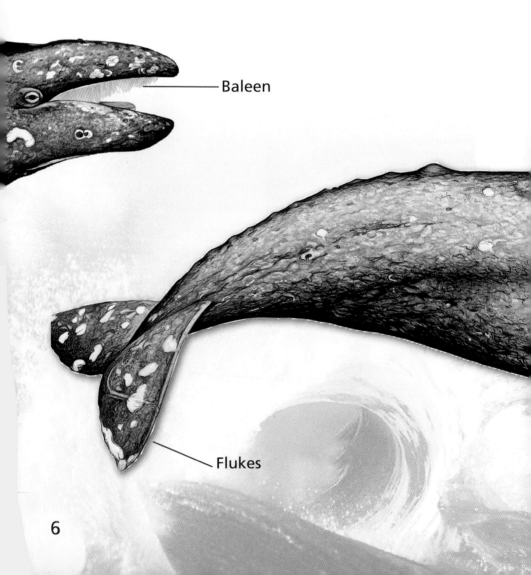

Baleen

Flukes

Gray whales are thirty-six to fifty feet long, and weigh sixteen to forty-five tons. One ton is equal to two thousand pounds. Males are smaller than females.

Whales are mammals that use blowholes to breathe. Gray whales have two blowholes on the tops of their heads. Protective flaps of muscle cover the blowholes just before the whale dives so that water cannot get in.

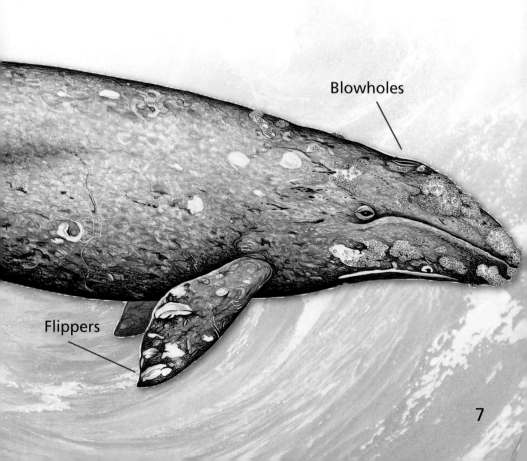

Blowholes

Flippers

Whales breathe when they come to the surface. They exhale warm, moist air from their blowholes. Then they take in fresh air. Vapor forms when the warm, exhaled air meets the cool ocean air. This vapor is called the blow. The gray whale's blow looks heart shaped when seen from the front or back.

Gray whales often show their flukes, the two halves of the tail, before they dive. Their wide tail helps them dive deep down. Whales use their flippers to turn and to stop while swimming.

Whales come to the surface to breathe.

Gray whales do not have teeth. They have baleen. Baleen is made of keratin. Your fingernails are also made of keratin. Baleen plates look like grayish, yellowish bristles. About 160 baleen plates hang from each side of the whale's upper jaw.

Baleen

This gray whale shows its baleen.

CHAPTER THREE
How do gray whales eat?

Gray whales dive to the ocean floor to eat. They roll on their sides. They suck up mouthfuls of water and mud. The baleen filters out tiny, shrimplike animals as they spit out the mud. The whales use their tongues to loosen the animals from the baleen. Then they swallow the food whole.

Gray whales feed on the bottom of the ocean.

Gray whales eat creatures such as this amphipod.

Gray whales have a summer feeding season. An adult gray whale eats about twenty-six hundred pounds every day during summer. Gray whales eat little, or nothing at all, for the rest of the year. They survive off their layer of blubber, or fat, that has been built up during the summer months.

This gray whale is feeding.

CHAPTER FOUR

How do gray whales migrate?

Gray whales travel about twelve thousand miles every year. This is the longest known migration, or movement from one place to another, of any mammal. They swim along the west coast of Canada, the United States, and Mexico. Gray whales travel within a few hundred yards of the coast. People enjoy standing on coastal **bluffs** to watch the whales migrate.

Gray whales leave the cold northern waters in mid-October. Pregnant females are the first to leave. They arrive in warm waters in time to give birth. Other gray whales follow.

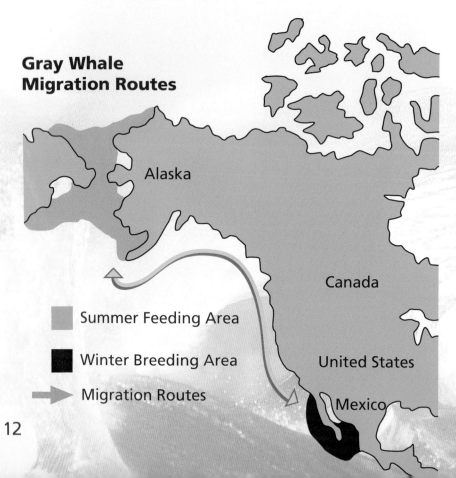

Gray Whale Migration Routes

Alaska

Canada

United States

Mexico

Summer Feeding Area

Winter Breeding Area

Migration Routes

Most of the gray whales arrive in the warm, **tropical** waters near Mexico between December and January. Many spend the winter in lagoons. A **lagoon** is a small body of water connected to a larger body of water. The whales give birth, breed, play, and raise the calves. They begin to migrate north in late February. Mothers and calves may not leave until April or May.

Gray whale and calf

CHAPTER FIVE

How do gray whales communicate?

Gray whales make moaning, **rumbling,** and grunting sounds. Their sounds may help to attract mates or to keep track of their calves.

Breaching is thought to be another form of communication. Breaching is when the whales hurl themselves out of the water. Then they plunge back in with a splash. Breaching may be related to breeding. It may also help clean off the lice and barnacles on a whale's skin. Or it might simply be a form of play.

This gray whale is breaching.

Whales are sensitive to touch. They are also curious, smart, and playful. Beginning in the 1970s, gray whales began approaching small boats. The friendly whales allowed humans to stroke their skin, rub their baleen, or even kiss them. Gray whales are beautiful. Maybe one day you will be a whale watcher!

Whale watchers touch a gray whale.

Glossary

biologists *n.* scientists who study living things, including their origins, structures, activities, and distribution.

bluffs *n.* high, steep slopes or cliffs.

lagoon *n.* a pond or small lake, especially one connected with a larger body of water.

massive *adj.* big and heavy; bulky.

rumbling *adj.* making a deep, heavy, continuous sound.

tropical *adj.* of or like the regions 23.45 degrees north and south of the equator where the Sun can shine directly overhead.